Meet the rangers. Can you find all of us in the book?

Belinda

Bongane

Charity

Collet

Cute

Debra

Goodness

Leitah

Lerato

Loveness

Mirren

Naledi

Nocry

Nurse

Qolile

Remember

Rethabile

Tsakane

Vongani

Yenzekile

Millbrook Press™
An imprint of Lerner Publishing Group, Inc.
241 First Avenue North
Minneapolis, MN 55401 USA

For reading levels and more information, look up this title at www.lernerbooks.com.

Additional image credits: Umoya Khulula Wildlife Rehabilitation Centre, p. 7 (bottom left); Dr. Louise Swemmer, p. 14 (bottom right); Lotty - PANGO & LINN, p. 25.

Designed by Danielle Carnito.
Main body text set in Conduit ITC Std.
Typeface provided by International Typeface Corporation.

Library of Congress Cataloging-in-Publication Data

Names: Crull, Kelly, author.
Title: The Black Mambas : the world's first all-woman anti-poaching unit / Kelly Crull.
Other titles: World's first all-woman anti-poaching unit
Description: Minneapolis : Millbrook Press, [2025] | Audience: Ages 6–10 | Audience: Grades 4–6 | Summary: "Go on patrol with the Black Mambas, South Africa's first women-led anti-poaching unit. Meet the rangers and discover all they do to protect the wildlife at the Olifants West Nature Reserve." Provided by publisher.
Identifiers: LCCN 2024023805 (print) | LCCN 2024023806 (ebook) | ISBN 9798765627259 (library binding) | ISBN 9798765659199 (epub)
Subjects: LCSH: Black Mambas (Anti-poaching unit) | Park rangers—South Africa—Olifants West Nature Reserve. | Game protection—South Africa—Olifants West Nature Reserve. | Olifants West Nature Reserve (South Africa)
Classification: LCC SK575.S5 C78 2025 (print) | LCC SK575.S5 (ebook) | DDC 639.90968—dc23/eng/20240601

LC record available at https://lccn.loc.gov/2024023805
LC ebook record available at https://lccn.loc.gov/2024023806

Manufactured in the United States of America
2-1013801-52107-2/18/2026

Acknowledgments

This book would not have been possible without my team: my family, April, Alleke, Teo, and Ruben, who have always believed in me; Deborah Warren at East West Literary Agency; Jesseca Fusco, Danielle Carnito, and Carol Hinz at Lerner Publishing Group who edited and designed the book; the folks at Transfrontier Africa, specifically Valeria van der Westhuizen for her dedication and countless hours coordinating my trip and interviews, collecting data, and fact-checking, and Craig Spencer for his vision and leadership; the Hoedspruit Reptile Centre for assisting me in photographing their black mambas; Three Bridges Restaurant, Pub, and B&B for your hospitality and excellent meals; Megan Ribbens and her family for welcoming me to South Africa; and, of course, the rangers of the Black Mamba Anti-Poaching Unit. You are my heroes!

Source Notes

3 Leitah Mkhabela, interview with the author, November 26, 2021.
5 Collet Ngobeni, interview with the author, August 20, 2021.
7 Vongani Masingi, interview with the author, September 21, 2021.
8 Belinda Acacia Mzimba, interview with the author, November 8, 2024.
9 Mhlongo.
10 Naledi Malungane, interview with the author, December 7, 2023.
12 Black Mambas, "Code of Honor," inspired by Charlene van der Berg, "Code of Honour," 2019.
17 Ngobeni, interview.
19 Masingi, interview.
21 Nkateko Letti Mzimba, interview with the author, September 8, 2021.
21 Mhlongo, interview.
21 Mzimba, interview.
21 Masingi, interview.
22 Mkhabela, interview, February 23, 2022.
25 Mhlongo, interview.
28 Masingi, interview.
34 Mkhabela, interview, February 23, 2022.
36 Collet Ngobeni, "Black Mamba Anti-Poaching Unit - 2015 Champions of the Earth Acceptance Speech," YouTube video, UN Environment Programme, posted October 8, 2015, https://youtu.be/DIEXrw-xgxY?si=4VJjLGULC-9 PvvP.

Cover Leitah Mkhabela, interview with the author, February 23, 2022.
Cover Ngobeni, interview.

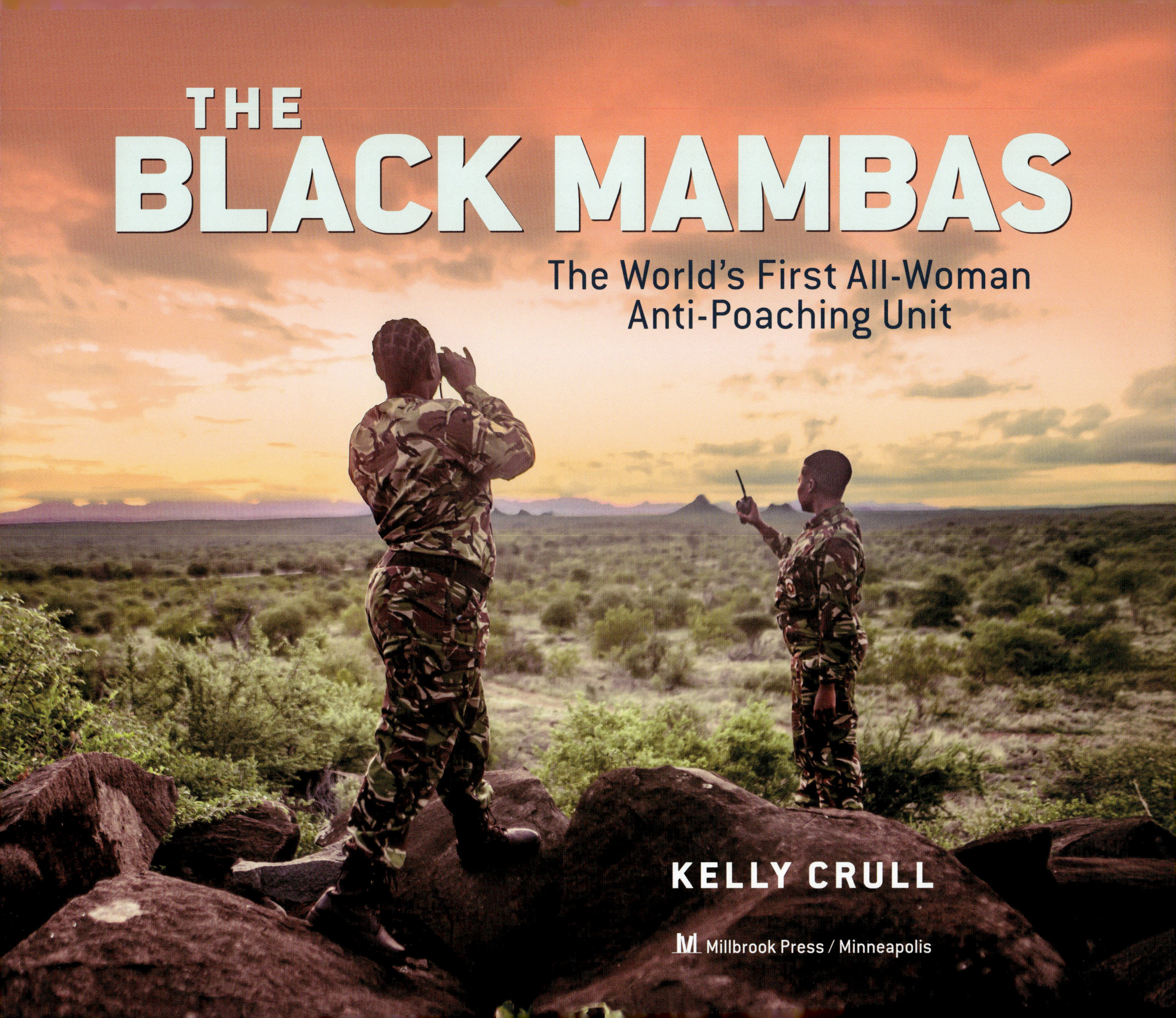

THE
BLACK MAMBAS
The World's First All-Woman
Anti-Poaching Unit
KELLY CRULL
Millbrook Press / Minneapolis

We are the Black Mambas!

We are the first women park rangers in South Africa and the first women-led anti-poaching unit in the world.

Although we come from different tribes and speak different languages, we are united by a common goal. We want to protect the wildlife in our reserve!

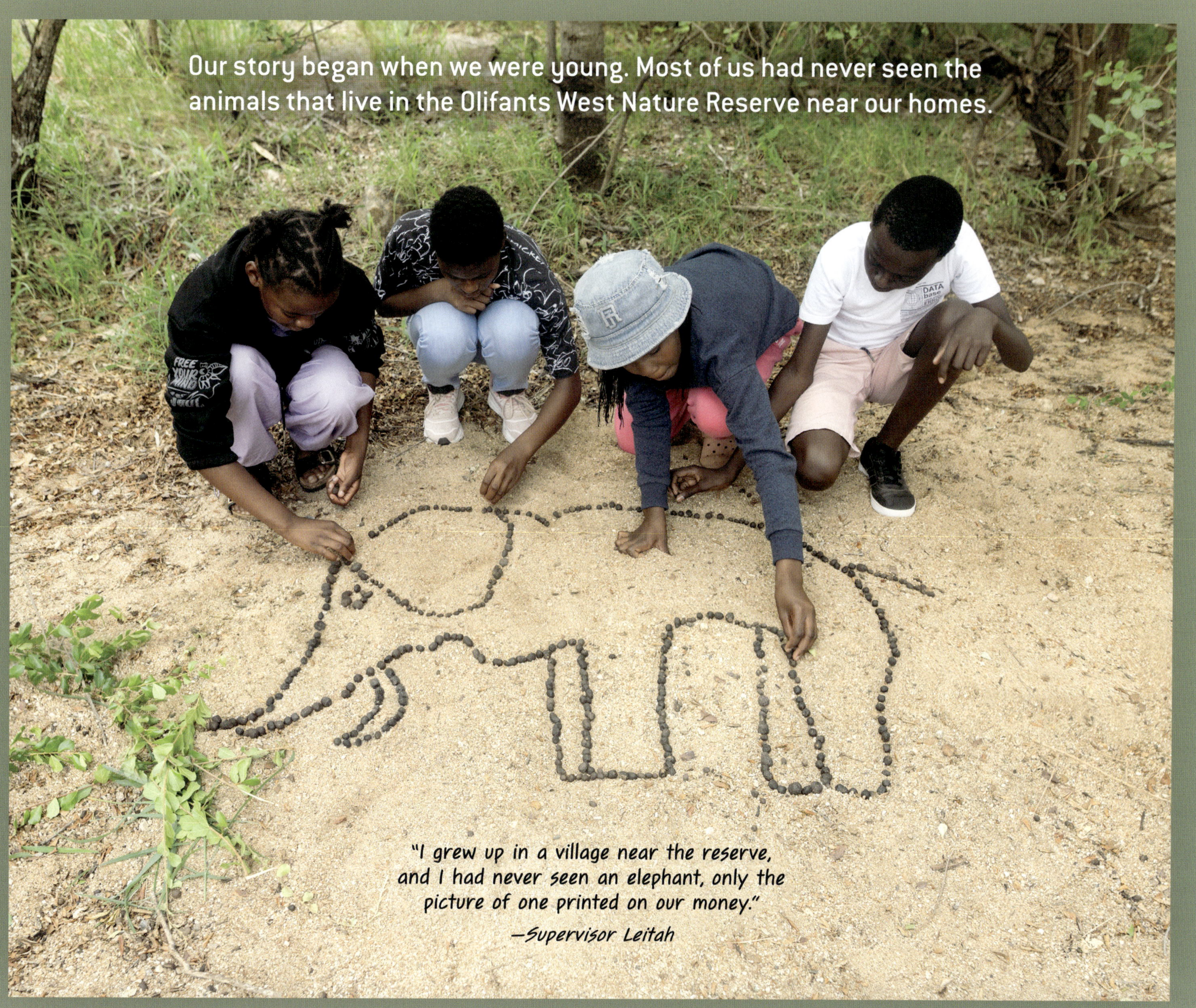

Our story began when we were young. Most of us had never seen the animals that live in the Olifants West Nature Reserve near our homes.

"I grew up in a village near the reserve, and I had never seen an elephant, only the picture of one printed on our money."
—Supervisor Leitah

When we finally met our neighbors, we discovered that they're a lot like us.

They have families. They like to cuddle and play games. They get hungry and tired. Sometimes they argue. They stick together.

But the animals in the reserve began to disappear, especially the rhinos and the pangolins.

OLIFANTS WEST NATURE RESERVE is part of the Greater Kruger National Park, home to the largest population of white rhinos and some critically endangered black rhinos. In the past fifteen years, eight out of every ten rhinos in Kruger have disappeared. That is a loss of one rhino every day. The main threat to these rhinos is poaching.

The men from our villages who are poachers sneak into the reserve at night and kill the animals. They take parts of the animals with them to sell or eat. They believe poaching is the best way to provide for their families.

PANGOLINS ARE THE WORLD'S ONLY SCALED MAMMAL. Poachers kill more of them than any other mammal. By the time you finish reading this book, a pangolin will be poached from the wild. Along with rhino horns, pangolin scales and claws are worth a lot of money in illegal markets. They are used in traditional medicine, even though there is no proof that this practice works. They are made of keratin, the same material as your fingernails.

We found another way to feed our families.

When we heard the reserve was hiring women to become the first female rangers in South Africa, we were first in line. Our job is to protect the animals in the reserve from poachers.

"I am from a community near the reserve. When lions, warthogs, or impalas entered our village, we used to kill them. Now we understand their importance, so we just chase them back into the reserve. I tell my neighbors they don't need to go poaching because these animals create jobs. Tourists come from other countries to see them, creating work for field guides, taxi drivers, chefs, housekeepers, and rangers. Protecting the environment brings more jobs."

—Sergeant Belinda

Our families weren't as excited as we were. They wondered if women could do a job that has always been done by men. They wondered what other people would think. They wondered if we would be safe.
"We were told this job was only for men, but we've proved that women can do this job too."
—Sergeant Cute

When we arrived on our first day on the job, we discovered that we were not alone. We are part of a sisterhood!

We named ourselves the Black Mambas after the most feared snake in South Africa. Together, we are strong and brave enough to take on any challenge.

DID YOU NOTICE THAT THE BLACK MAMBA IS NOT ACTUALLY BLACK? Its name comes from the black inside of its mouth. It is one of the most dangerous snakes in the world, and just two drops of its venom can kill a person. Like most snakes, though, a black mamba will avoid people when possible and would rather hide or escape than bite someone.

Our job begins with a parade. We recite the Black Mambas Code of Honor.

Stand proud and say these words with us . . .

CODE OF HONOR

I am a Mamba hear me clear,
Poachers be warned, I have no fear.
Fauna and flora I pledge to protect,
There is always something to detect.
Eyes and ears serve the ground,
Here and there and all around.
From dusk till dawn, this promise I keep,
Protect the voiceless while they sleep.
Sister to my left, sister to my right,
We stand together in this plight.
We stand with pride and unity,
Uplifting our community.
Empower mothers to educate,
Our young Nature Guardians are at stake.
Honesty and integrity are what we strive
While we keep our heritage alive.
I am a Mamba. Let this be clear!

Now it's time for our workout! Two or three times a week, we run 3 miles (5 km), do push-ups and sit-ups, and complete an obstacle course.

Ready, set, go!

We practice survival skills.
We need to be able to survive
without food or water.

HAVE YOU HEARD OF THE RULE OF THREES?
Generally, a person can survive for three minutes
in icy water or without breathing, three hours
without shelter in extreme heat or cold, three days
without water, and three weeks without food.

SHELTER

We find shelter in an area
surrounded by thorny
bushes to protect us from
lions. We lean branches
against a fallen tree to shade
us from the hot sun.

WATER

We find water by following animal
tracks to a stream or water hole.
Green trees or bushes are other
signs that water may be nearby.
Before drinking, we boil the water
over a fire to kill any germs.

FOOD

Usually, we won't need to find food. Our
bodies store fat we can use to survive.
The easiest, most nutritious food to
find is insects, such as mopane worms.
We avoid spiders, and we don't eat
plants unless we know they're safe.

We navigate the reserve
using a map and compass.

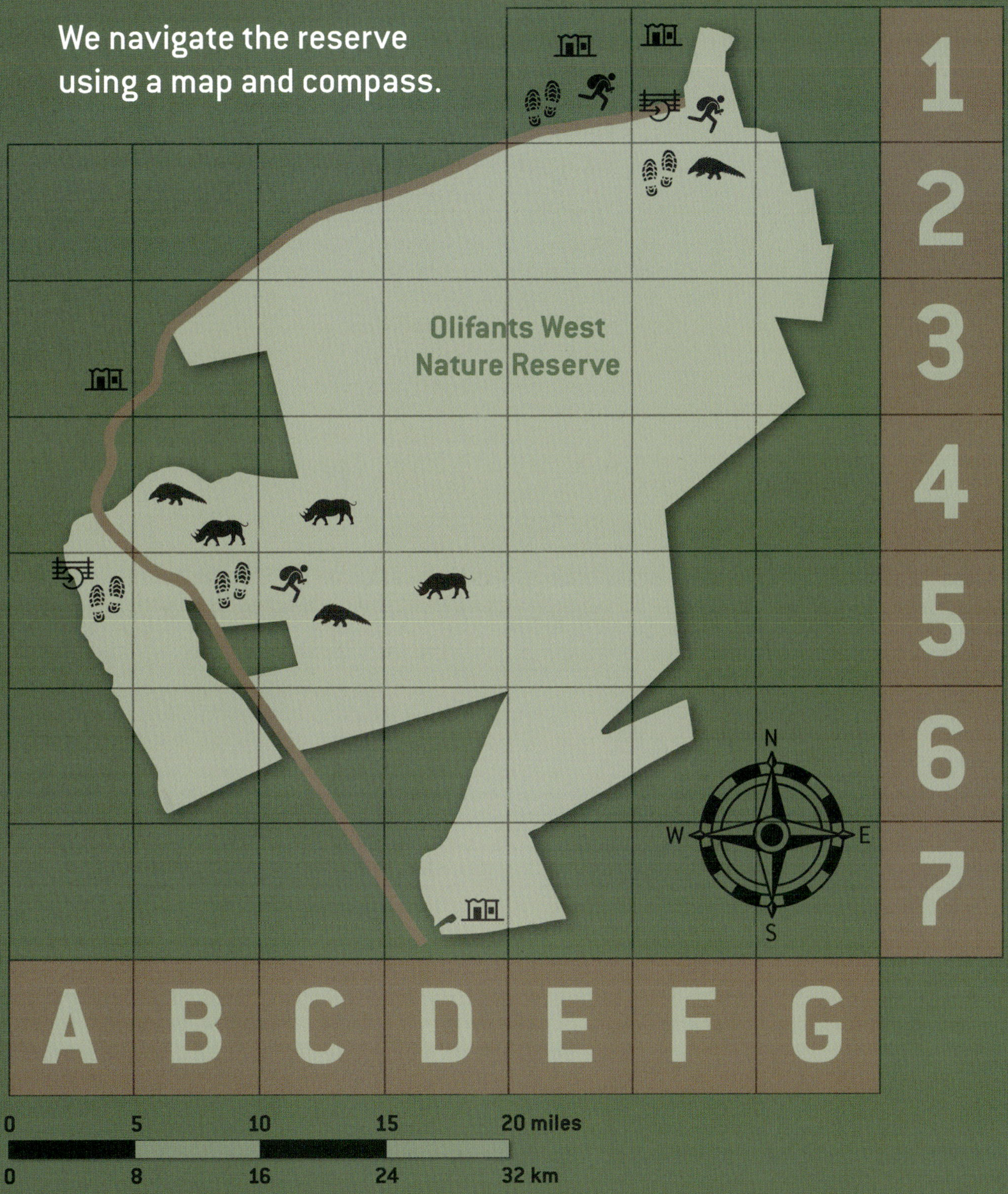

Olifants West
Nature Reserve

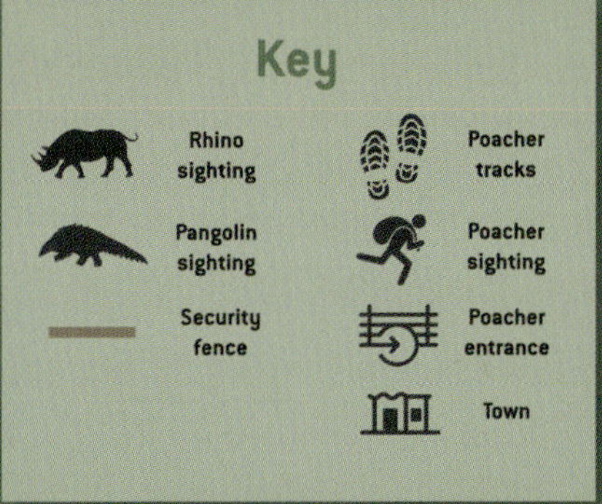

TWO TEAMS OF RANGERS ARE HEADING OUT ON MORNING FOOT PATROL. They need your help to plan their routes.

1. Use the map key to locate the animals the rangers need to protect.

2. Look for the poachers' recent activity on the map. Where should the rangers be looking for poachers?

3. Check the scale in the bottom corner of the page. Keep in mind that each team walks 10 miles (16 km) on patrol. They also prefer to walk along the fence, so they can check for holes where poachers may have entered the reserve.

4. Use the letters along the bottom of the map and the numbers along the side to create grid coordinates (for example, C2) for each team's route.

Twice a day, we patrol the reserve.

We look for signs of poachers.

holes in the fence

litter

footprints

"We walk along the fence and look for holes. Warthogs dig under the fence, and poachers use these holes to enter the reserve. The reserve is very big, so poachers mark their route with reflective tape, small flags, or plastic, so they can find their way out again. The most obvious sign a poacher is in the reserve is their footprints."

—*Supervisor Collet*

The best part about being on patrol is seeing the wildlife.

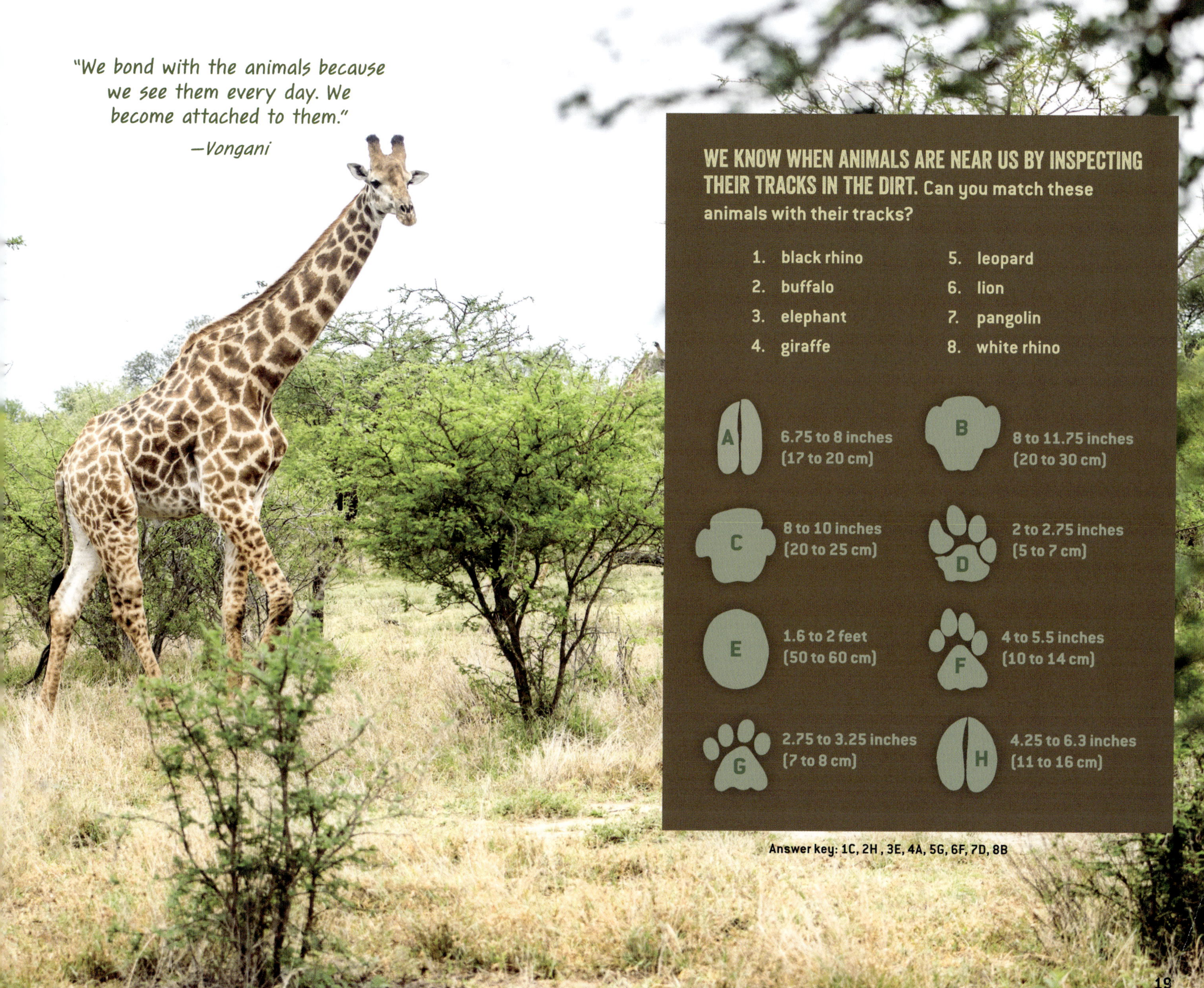
"We bond with the animals because we see them every day. We become attached to them."
—Vongani

WE KNOW WHEN ANIMALS ARE NEAR US BY INSPECTING THEIR TRACKS IN THE DIRT. Can you match these animals with their tracks?

1. black rhino
2. buffalo
3. elephant
4. giraffe
5. leopard
6. lion
7. pangolin
8. white rhino

A 6.75 to 8 inches (17 to 20 cm)
B 8 to 11.75 inches (20 to 30 cm)
C 8 to 10 inches (20 to 25 cm)
D 2 to 2.75 inches (5 to 7 cm)
E 1.6 to 2 feet (50 to 60 cm)
F 4 to 5.5 inches (10 to 14 cm)
G 2.75 to 3.25 inches (7 to 8 cm)
H 4.25 to 6.3 inches (11 to 16 cm)

Answer key: 1C, 2H , 3E, 4A, 5G, 6F, 7D, 8B

Even though we feel connected to the animals in the reserve, we still need to be careful around them. We stay safe by watching the animals closely.

"Giraffes are my favorite animal. They have long necks, so they can see if any predators are nearby. If I am by a giraffe, I know I am safe."

—Sergeant Nkateko

"We must be quiet around elephants because they do not like noise. Once, we faced a large, aggressive male. He charged us, but we stayed together and faced him. He stopped six feet [2 m] away, sniffed us, and left."

—Sergeant Cute

"When you see a rhino, look carefully to see if it is a white or black rhino. White rhinos are social and less aggressive. Black rhinos are solitary, very territorial, and more aggressive. If you see a black rhino, you need to hide behind a tree or escape. Otherwise, it will charge you."

—Sergeant Nkateko

"Faced with a lion, stand your ground and keep eye contact. Don't turn around, don't back up, and most importantly, don't run away, or you risk becoming prey and dying."

—Vongani

We search the bush for snares. A snare is a wire used by poachers to trap animals. We remove the snares, so they can't injure more animals.

Can you find all four snares in this area?

"Poachers place snares mostly around water holes. They use vegetation on pathways to place their snares, so the animals are easily trapped."
—Supervisor Leitah

THE BLACK MAMBAS USE THEIR PHONES to record observations about the animals in the reserve, such as the kind of animal, number, gender, age, and health. They also record signs of poachers such as holes in the fence, footprints, snares, killed or injured animals, and poacher sightings. This data helps them plan future patrol routes.

When we find animals that poachers have captured, we bring the animals to a veterinarian. The vet helps make sure the animals are healthy enough to return to the wild.

Some animals, like this pangolin, are tagged with a radio transmitter before being released back into the reserve. The radio transmitters emit a signal the rangers use to regularly check on the animals in case they need help.

We set up roadblocks to inspect vehicles as they enter or exit the reserve.

THE RANGERS SEARCH FOR ITEMS THAT HAVE BEEN POACHED:
rhino horn
pangolin scales
bushmeat
plants
firewood

In the ops room, we monitor surveillance cameras, communicate with rangers on patrol, and notify the police when we find poachers in the reserve.

We use walkie-talkies to communicate.

Back on patrol, we find a hole in the fence.

We notice footprints nearby and follow them deep into the bush.

"If the outline is quite visible, the track is fresh. It could be less than twenty-four hours old. But if the outline is not very visible, this could be an old track."

—Vongani

We discover a bushmeat kitchen. Poachers have killed animals in the reserve. They have left meat to dry, so it will not spoil and is easier to carry home or to the market. Their camp has . . .

We collect evidence and send photos to the ops room.

The rangers in the ops room plan an ambush.

After dark, we hide near the hole in the fence and
wait for the poachers to return to their camp.

It's almost midnight when we see a flashlight . . .

We notify another team of rangers that the poachers are headed their way.

The rangers are waiting for the poachers at the camp. They arrest the poachers, and we turn them over to the police so they cannot hurt any more animals.

Working together, we have made the Olifants West Nature Reserve one of the most difficult places to poach animals.

"I am like a mother to the wild animals. A mother protects her child, and I protect these animals."
—Supervisor Leitah

97,371
miles (156,704 km)
patrolled in 2020–2023

1,274
poacher activities reported
by rangers in 2020–2023

1,685
snares removed in
2016–2024

138
roadblocks in
2020–2023

3,771
days of wildlife protection
in 2013–2024

We've been recognized around the world for our achievements. In 2015 we received the United Nations Champions of the Earth award.

"It is a great honor and privilege to receive this prestigious award on behalf of the Black Mambas anti-poaching unit. I am humbled and grateful for the recognition from the United Nations."
—Supervisor Collet

But we feel proudest when we invite the children from our villages to visit the reserve. Here, they meet their wild neighbors—just as we did when we were young.

Instead of telling the children these animals are disappearing, we get to tell them that we are keeping the animals safe from poachers.

We say to the animals in the reserve . . .
We are your mothers, your aunties, and your sisters.
We are here to protect you.

The Black Mambas are on patrol!

Meet the Animals

Here is how to pronounce the name of each animal in Sepedi, a language the Black Mambas use in their villages:

kgwara
(kuh-WAH-ruh)
pangolin

kubu
(KOO-boo)
hippopotamus

nare
(NAH-ray)
buffalo

phiri
(PEE-ree)
hyena

pitsi
(PEET-see)
zebra

tau
(tao)
lion

thutlwa
(TWO-twa)
giraffe

tlou
(tow)
elephant

tšhukudu
(chew-COO-doo)
rhino

NATO Phonetic Alphabet

The rangers spell important words with the NATO Phonetic Alphabet. Duke, the name of a rhino in the reserve, is spelled Delta-Uniform-Kilo-Echo. Can you spell your name using this alphabet?

Alpha
Bravo
Charlie
Delta
Echo
Foxtrot
Golf

Hotel
India
Juliett
Kilo
Lima
Mike
November

Oscar
Papa
Quebec
Romeo
Sierra
Tango
Uniform

Victor
Whiskey
X-ray
Yankee
Zulu

Author's Note

I spent five years learning about the Black Mambas while I worked on this book. I read articles, listened to podcasts, looked at photos, and watched videos about the rangers. I interviewed them on the phone. I talked with their friends, families, and coworkers. Best of all, I got to visit the Black Mambas in South Africa. I got up early to walk the fence, and late at night I scanned the bush with a flashlight from the back of their truck. I swept the bush for snares. I listened. I observed. I asked questions. I took lots of pictures. And together, we told their story. Most of the words in this book are taken directly from my conversations with them.

I learned many things from the rangers, but the most remarkable was their ability to see things I did not. In a spot I would have passed by without a second glance, they noticed a family of rhinos on a hill, a leopard hiding in the bushes, a small cat perched in a tree, and lions lounging in the grass.

The rangers' job is to be the eyes and ears of the reserve. Thanks to this "visual policing," no rhinos have been poached in Olifants West Nature Reserve since 2013. The rangers also notice snares in the bush. According to the local game warden, snares kill more animals than anything else. And the Black Mambas have reduced snared wildlife in their reserve by 86 percent.

The first and most important step to protect wildlife is to get to know our wild neighbors. Look for them. Learn their names. Find out where they live, what they eat, when their bedtime is, how they have fun, and who their friends and family are. The more you know about your neighbors, the more you will care about them. Ask grown-ups what you can do to help your neighbors grow and stay safe. Keep asking until someone answers your questions.

I decided to copy the Black Mambas and practice noticing wildlife. Even though I live in a city, I noticed all kinds of wildlife I had never seen before. I didn't even know a family of foxes is living in my backyard!

I also noticed other people who care for wildlife in my community. One of my students, Sonja, recently told me that sometimes she rides around her neighborhood after school and looks for birds that are hurt or abandoned. She has rescued dozens of birds, which she brings to the bird rehabilitation center where she volunteers. Sonja started saving birds when she was ten. Sonja is a conservation hero like the Black Mambas. But she is also an ordinary person like you and me. I wonder what extraordinary thing you might decide to do today.

Further Information

BOOKS

Estes, Richard D. *The Safari Companion: A Guide to Watching African Mammals*. New York: Chelsea Green Publishing, 1999. Meet the animals that the rangers see every day on patrol and learn how they live, play, and survive in the wild.

Eszterhas, Suzi. *Operation Pangolin: Saving the World's Only Scaled Mammal*. Minneapolis: Millbrook Press, 2022. Learn more about pangolins, one of the most poached animals, and the rescuers and researchers that protect them.

Markle, Sandra. *The Great Rhino Rescue: Saving the Southern White Rhino*. Minneapolis: Millbrook Press, 2019. Find out how civilians, volunteer organizations, and African governments are working together to protect rhinos.

Stuart, Chris, and Mathilde Stuart. *A Field Guide to the Tracks & Signs of Southern, Central & East African Wildlife*, 4th ed. Cape Town: Struik Nature, 2013. The rangers use this book and others recommended by the Field Guides Association of South Africa to identify tracks and other animal behaviors.

WEBSITES

Africam Live African Wildlife Safari Streams
https://www.africam.com/wildlife/live-african-wildlife-safari-streams
Join the Black Mambas on patrol as a virtual ranger. You can help protect the wildlife in the reserve by watching these live streams.

Black Mambas Official Website
https://transfrontierafrica.org/blackmambas
Visit the Black Mambas website for their latest news, photos, and videos and to subscribe to their newsletter.

Black Mambas YouTube Playlist
https://kellycrull.com/blackmambas/playlist
The rangers have put together a playlist for you with their favorite Black Mambas videos!

Bush Babies Environmental Education Program
https://transfrontierafrica.org/bushbabies
The rangers love kids! They regularly visit schools near the reserve and lead field trips to the bush. Follow them on social media to see how the students care for plants and wildlife.

Virtual Author Visit
https://kellycrull.com/blackmambas/visit
Join the author behind the scenes as he answers some common questions about researching and writing this book and tells stories about visiting the Black Mambas in person.